FAMILY

Jokes & Riddles

By Jeffrey S. Nelsen

CHECKERBOARD PRESS ❖ NEW YORK

Does your mom darn socks?

No, but you should hear my dad when his car won't start!

What do computer programmers go to the dentist for?

Overbyte.

2

Why are sons 52 times more important than fathers?

Because Father's Day comes only once a year, but Son-day comes once every week.

How do space families travel?

In space station wagons.

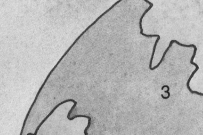

What do you call a sister who's always nice, bakes cookies for you, and never bothers you?

Somebody else's.

3

Does your dad have a bicycle?

No. He rides a pop-cycle.

Why is there no cat in a computer age family's house?

Because they prefer to have a mouse.

If your dad was a rattlesnake
and your mom was a thief,
what would you be?

A rattle-sneak.

What do you call an ancestral comb?

A family hair-loom.

RATTLE
RATTLE

What kind of family tree are army babies born into?

An infant-tree.

How do computer families eat?

One byte at a time.

If your dad was a truck and your mom was a pig, what would you be?

An 18 squealer.

How do genie children get to school?

In a flying car pool.

Why do country-and-western families always pay attention to a horn?

Because it's usually attached to a bull.

What card game do country-and-western families like to play?

Cow-poker.

Why did the general's baby stop drinking milk?

He had bottle fatigue.

What did the computer couple name their baby boy?

Chip.

Why couldn't the sergeant take his kids to the movies?

Because they were rated for general audiences only.

9

Why did the king move his family to another kingdom?

He wanted them to have a change of subjects.

What did the prince do when he was turned into a frog?

Nothing. He was rivet-rivet-ed to his seat.

Why are witch families such good workers?

Because they're always willing
to spell one another.

What do witches' children inherit?

Family heir-brooms.

If your uncle was a vampire, what would you be?

A blood relative.

Seymour Vampire III
"Uncle Vampie"

Do doctors make good parents?

Yes, they have a lot of patients.

What snacks do computer scientists' families like to eat?

Microchip cookies.

What do you call a family of ducks that likes soft drinks?

Soda quackers.

What do clumsy families and families that like to travel have in common?

They both have a lot of trips.

Do monster families eat dinner with their neighbors?

No. They eat their neighbors first.
THEN they eat their dinner.

How do snake parents
punish their children?

They take away
their rattles.

mashed
potatoes

Salad

Milk

neighbors

Why did the clown bury his wife's feet and pour water on her head?

He wanted to start a family tree.

What do you call a blanket that covers a family of hoboes?

A bum wrap.

What do you call a family of crooks that lives next door?

Neighbor-hoods.

How do porcupines carry their babies?

Very carefully.

If all your relatives lived in the same building, what would you call it?

A family tree house.

What kind of vegetables do families of giants like to eat?

Squash.

Why do computer families like to eat out?

They're menu driven.

18

What do bunny parents give their kids when they get sick?

Hare restorer.

What did the monkey say when his sister had a baby?

"Well, I'll be a monkey's uncle!"

What do you get when brothers and sisters have a party?

Sibling revelry.

What is a father's favorite tree?

A pop-lar.

What do you have
when your uncle's
wife raises chickens?

An aunt farm.

What happened when
the boy accidentally spilled
his dad's coffee?

His dad got son-burned.

What do you call it when your dad tells you a bad joke?

Pop-corn.

Why don't vampire children pass food to their parents at the dinner table?

Because you shouldn't feed the hand that bites you.

Why did the duck family decide not to have any more babies?

They had too many bills.

What would you call Dracula's son?

A little nipper.

How well do a sea captain's kids do in school?

They're usually at C level.

What do horse parents read to their children at bedtime?

Pony-tales.

What's another name for things a baby throws around?

Kiddie litter.